GRAPHIC LIBRARY®

GRAPHIC SCIENCE

A CRASH COURSE in FORCES AND MOTION

WITH MAX AXIOM SUPER SCIENTIST

by Emily Sohn

illustrated by Steve Erwin

and Charles Barnett III

Consultant:
Dr. Ronald Browne
Associate Professor of Elementary Edu
Minnesota State University, Manka

D1207898

Graphic Library is published by Capstone Press,
1710 Roe Crest Drive, North Mankato, Minnesota 56003
www.capstonepub.com

Library of Congress Cataloging-in-Publication Data
Sohn, Emily.
    A crash course in forces and motion with Max Axiom, super scientist / by Emily Sohn;
illustrated by Steve Erwin and Charles Barnett III.
        p. cm.—(Graphic library. graphic science)
    Summary: "In graphic novel format, follows the adventures of Max Axiom as he
explains the science behind forces and motion"—Provided by publisher.
    Includes bibliographical references and index.
    ISBN-13: 978-0-7368-6837-2 (hardcover)
    ISBN-10: 0-7368-6837-2 (hardcover)
    ISBN-13: 978-0-7368-7890-6 (softcover pbk.)
    ISBN-10: 0-7368-7890-4 (softcover pbk.)
    1. Motion—Juvenile literature. 2. Force and energy—Juvenile literature.
3. Adventure stories—Juvenile literature. I. Erwin, Steve, ill. II. Barnett, Charles, III,
ill. III. Title. IV. Series.
QC133.5.S65 2007
531'.11—dc22   2006031801

Art Director and Designer
Bob Lentz and Thomas Emery

Cover Artist
Tod Smith

Storyboard Artist
Shannon Eric Denton

Colorist
Krista Ward

Editor
Christopher L. Harbo

TABLE of CONTENTS

In fact, the world is full of all kinds of motion.

Everything that moves needs a force to get it moving.

Back for another jump, already?

You bet!

A force is any push or pull on an object. Bungee jumping depends on a force called gravity.

It pulls objects toward each other, and it keeps us on the earth.

Gravity is the reason I fall down, not up or sideways.

Brakes on the roller coaster used friction to slow us down too. Come on, I'll show you how.

BRAKE RAIL

Each roller coaster car has two brake fins attached to its underside. As the cars approach the station, these fins slide between two sets of brake rails.

I see. When the brake rails squeeze against the fins, friction stops the cars.

I had a great time, Rosita, but I've got to run. My nephew is having his birthday party over at Skater's Paradise.

See you later, Max!

What's mass, Uncle Max?

Mass is the amount of matter in an object. The bowling ball has more matter in it than the tennis ball, so it feels heavier.

Think about it. Which ball would be easier to juggle, Nick?

GRAVITATIONAL PULL

ACCESS GRANTED: MAX AXIOM

Weight is different from mass. Weight is determined by gravity's pull on an object. Each planet in our solar system has a different gravitational pull. If you traveled to each of the places below, your mass would always be the same, but your weight would be different. Multiply your weight by the number shown below each planet to find out how much you would weigh there. If you weigh 100 pounds on earth, you would weigh 38 pounds on Mars and 236 pounds on Jupiter.

VENUS
.88

NEPTUNE
1.13

MARS
.38

SATURN
.92

JUPITER
2.36

THHRRRP!

THHRRRP!

THHRRRP!

Making balloons zip around is one of their favorite pastimes.

You like playing with spaceships, do you?

Spaceships? These are balloons.

But if the chain on a chair breaks, centripetal force no longer acts on the chair. The chair would fly off in a straight line.

Whoa!

Looks like it's our turn to ride.

Are you sure this ride is safe?

Whee!

Perfectly!

This ride is crazy, Uncle Max!

Just watch the penny I'm holding when we drop.

Whoa. The penny looks like it's just floating there.

It's magic!

Actually, it's science! We're in free fall, and so is the penny. We're all falling at the same speed, so the penny looks as weightless as we feel.

Do astronauts feel weightless in space because they are falling?

Yes. Orbit is a free fall in a circle.

EXIT

To feel the most speed on a roller coaster, sit in the last seat. It reaches the top of the hills just as the front of the roller coaster gains its top speed down the hills.

The motion of amusement park rides sometimes makes you feel sick. Swinging, spinning, or going around in loops causes your eyes and the fluid in your ears to send confusing signals to your brain. Your brain can't decide which way is up or down.

Forces that don't cause objects to move are balanced forces. A great example of balanced forces is the chair you're sitting on. As you sit on a chair, the force of gravity pulls your body downward. At the same time, the chair pushes upward on your body with an equal force. Without these forces in balance, the chair would break and you would find yourself sitting on the ground.

Friction actually slows down skydivers as they fall from an airplane. Air resistance is a form of friction that happens between air and an object moving through it. Even with air resistance, skydivers reach speeds of about 120 miles (193 kilometers) per hour during free falls.

The peregrine falcon is the fastest animal on earth. In a steep hunting dive, it can reach 200 miles (322 kilometers) per hour.

Inertia causes objects to stay at rest or keep moving until a force acts upon them. In a moving car, inertia can be dangerous. Your body moves at the same speed as the car. If the driver suddenly slams on the brakes, the car stops, but your body keeps moving forward. Your seat belt applies a force to stop your body's forward motion. It's the only thing that keeps you from flying through the windshield.

 If you're looking for the fastest horse on the merry-go-round, pick an outside horse. To complete the circle, it must cover more distance in the same amount of time as an inside horse.

MORE ABOUT

SUPER SCIENTIST

Real name: Maxwell J. Axiom
Hometown: Seattle, Washington
Height: 6' 1"   **Weight:** 192 lbs
Eyes: Brown   **Hair:** None

Super capabilities: Super intelligence; able to shrink to the size of an atom; sunglasses give x-ray vision; lab coat allows for travel through time and space.

Origin: Since birth, Max Axiom seemed destined for greatness. His mother, a marine biologist, taught her son about the mysteries of the sea. His father, a nuclear physicist and volunteer park ranger, schooled Max on the wonders of earth and sky.

One day on a wilderness hike, a megacharged lightning bolt struck Max with blinding fury. When he awoke, Max discovered a newfound energy and set out to learn as much about science as possible. He traveled the globe earning degrees in every aspect of the field. Upon his return, he was ready to share his knowledge and new identity with the world. He had become Max Axiom, Super Scientist.

GLOSSARY

acceleration (ak-sel-uh-RAY-shuhn)—the change in speed of a moving body

balance (BAL-uhnss)—a state when forces are equal

centripetal force (sen-TRIP-uh-tuhl FORS)—the force that pulls an object turning in a circle inward toward the center

friction (FRIK-shuhn)—a force created when two objects rub together; friction slows down objects.

gravity (GRAV-uh-tee)—a force that pulls objects with mass together; gravity increases as the mass of objects increases or objects get closer; gravity pulls objects down toward the center of earth.

inertia (in-UR-shuh)—an object's state in which the object stays at rest or keeps moving in the same direction until a greater force acts on the object

mass (MASS)—the amount of material in an object

orbit (OR-bit)—the path an object follows while circling another object in space

resistance (ri-ZISS-tuhnss)—a force that opposes or slows the motion of an object; friction is a form of resistance.

speed (SPEED)—how fast something moves; speed is a measure of the time it takes something to cover a certain distance.

weight (WATE)—a measurement of how heavy something is

READ MORE

Cooper, Christopher. *Forces and Motion: From Push to Shove.* Science Answers. Chicago: Heinemann Library, 2003.

Fullick, Ann. *Under Pressure: Forces.* Everyday Science. Chicago: Heinemann Library, 2005.

Phelan, Glen. *Newton's Laws.* Physical Science. Washington, D.C.: National Geographic Society, 2004.

Stille, Darlene R. *Motion.* Science Around Us. Chanhassen, Minn.: Child's World, 2005.

Welch, Catherine A. *Forces and Motion: A Question and Answer Book.* Questions and Answers: Physical Science. Mankato, Minn.: Capstone Press, 2006.

INTERNET SITES

FactHound offers a safe, fun way to find Internet sites related to this book. All of the sites on FactHound have been researched by our staff.

Here's how:
1. Visit *www.facthound.com*
2. Choose your grade level.
3. Type in this book ID **0736868372** for age-appropriate sites. You may also browse subjects by clicking on letters, or by clicking on pictures and words.
4. Click on the **Fetch It** button.

FactHound will fetch the best sites for you!

Index